Eating Well

by Melanie Mitchell

Series consultants: Sonja Green, MD, and
Distinguished Professor Emerita Ann Nolte, PhD,
Department of Health Sciences, Illinois State University

Lerner Publications Company • Minneapolis

Daily serving recommendations in this book are based on the 2005 USDA diet guidelines for moderately active children ages 4 to 8 years old.

The MyPyramid symbol appears courtesy of the U.S. Department of Agriculture. USDA does not endorse any products, services, or organizations.

Lerner Publications Company
A division of Lerner Publishing Group
241 First Avenue North
Minneapolis, MN 55401 U.S.A.

Website address: www.lernerbooks.com

Words in **bold type** are explained in a glossary on page 31.

Library of Congress Cataloging-in-Publication Data

Mitchell, Melanie (Melanie S.).
    Eating well / by Melanie Mitchell.
      p. cm. — (Pull ahead books)
    Includes index.
    ISBN-13: 978-0-8225-2449-6 (lib. bdg. : alk. paper)
    ISBN-10: 0-8225-2449-X (lib. bdg. : alk. paper)
    1. Food. 2. Nutrition I. Title. II. Series.
TX353.M575 2006
613.2—dc22   2004028896

Manufactured in the United States of America
1 2 3 4 5 6 – JR – 11 10 09 08 07 06

There are so many kinds of foods to eat.

How can we choose the right foods
and eat well?

We can pick foods from the five food groups. The food guide MyPyramid shows these food groups.

We can pick a **variety** of foods. Eating food from each of the food groups helps us stay **healthy**.

We eat bread, cereal, rice, tortillas, and pasta. These are foods in the grains group.

The foods in the grains group give us lots of **energy**. People need energy to work and play each day.

Another food group is the vegetables
group. Broccoli and carrots are
vegetables. What are some others?

8

Fruit is another important food group.
Apples and bananas are fruit. What
fruit do you see here?

Vegetables and fruit give us **vitamins** and **minerals**. Vitamins and minerals help your body grow and stay healthy.

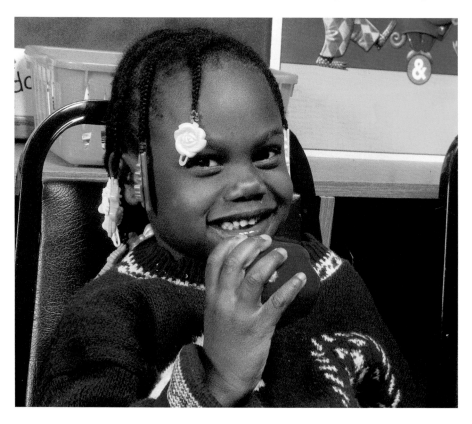

Some fruits, such as oranges, have vitamin C. We need vitamin C to help our skin and bodies heal.

Another food group is the milk group. It has foods like milk, cheese, and yogurt.

Foods made from milk have calcium.
Calcium makes bones strong.

The meat and beans group has foods like meat, **poultry**, fish, beans, eggs, and nuts. These foods have **protein**. It helps keep you strong.

Oils are in some foods. Salad dressing and cooking oil are kinds of oils.

Eating too little or too much of some foods is not healthy. How can we eat the right amount?

One way is to follow MyPyramid. It shows how much we need from each food group.

Children need about 3 to 5 ounces of grain foods a day.

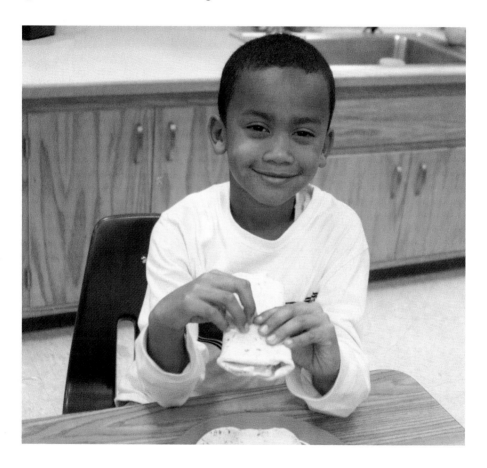

One slice of bread equals 1 ounce
from the grains group. So does one
tortilla or one-half cup of rice.

You should eat about 1 1/2 cups of vegetables a day. One sweet potato is a cup of vegetables. So are three spears of broccoli.

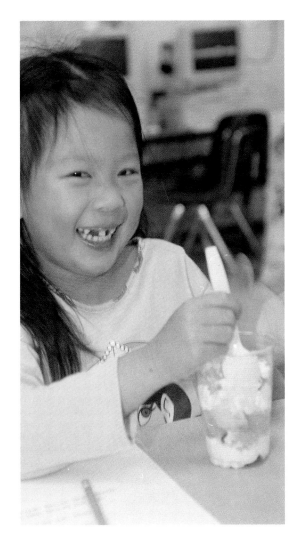

You need a little more than 1 cup of fruit a day. People can eat fresh fruit or canned fruit or drink fruit juice to stay healthy.

You should have about 2 to 3 cups of milk foods each day. This can be two cups of milk or two cups of yogurt.

You need 3 to 5 ounces from the meat and beans group each day. Each of these foods equals 3 ounces.

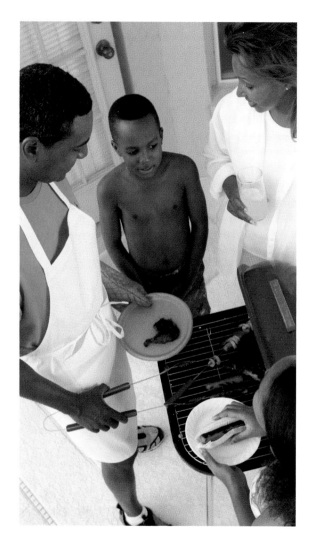

Meat with only a little fat is a good choice. Grilling, baking, or roasting meat cuts back on fat.

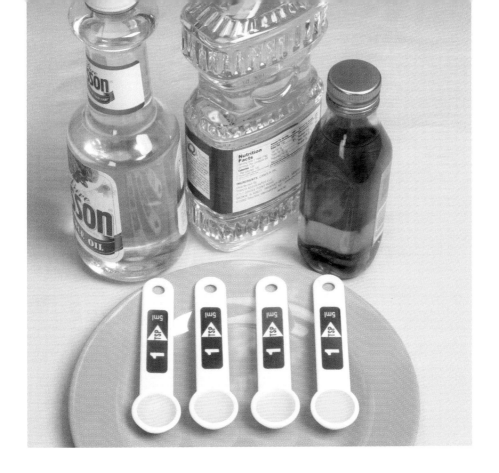

We get oils from some of the foods we eat. We need only a little bit of oils each day.

Food gives us energy to run and play.
Keeping active helps us use all the
food we eat.

Playing hard and eating a variety of foods keeps us healthy.

Did You Know that...?

■ Some vegetables have protein. Peanuts, soybeans, and black beans are in the vegetables group. But they also have protein. Foods like peanut butter or tofu or black beans and rice all have protein.

■ Whole grain foods are good for you. Whole wheat bread, oatmeal, and brown rice are kinds of whole wheat foods.

■ Vitamin A helps your eyes work. It can even help you see better at night! Carrots and sweet potatoes have vitamin A.

■ Your body needs iron. Iron is a mineral in food. It helps your body use **oxygen** and gives you energy. Iron is in broccoli, potato skins, raisins, beef, and tuna fish.

■ Some foods contain most of the food groups. A taco can be made with a tortilla, lettuce, tomatoes, cheese, and beans. Can you think of any other foods that have something from nearly all the food groups?

MyPyramid for Kids

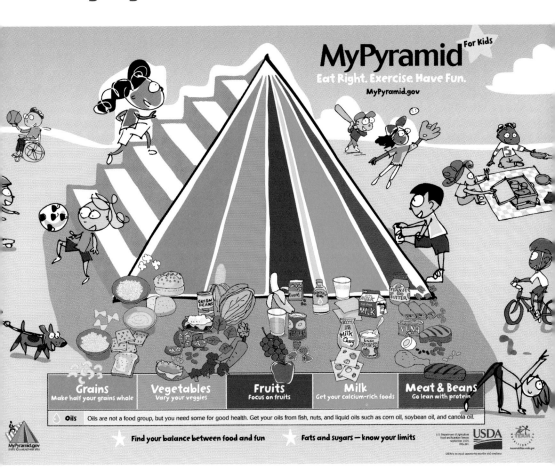

Books and Websites

Books

Rockwell, Lizzy. *Good Enough to Eat: A Kid's Guide to Food and Nutrition.* New York: HarperCollins Publishers, 1999.

Sears, William, and Martha Sears. *Eat Healthy, Feel Great.* Boston: Little, Brown & Company, 2002.

Websites

MyPyramid Blast Off Game
http://www.mypyramid.gov/kids/kids_game.html

Powerful Bones, Powerful Girls.
http://www.cdc.gov/powerfulbones/

Steps to a Healthier You—MyPyramid.gov
http://www.mypyramid.gov/

What Are Vitamins?—KidsHealth
http://www.kidshealth.org/kid/stay_healthy/food/vitamin.html

What's the Right Weight for Me?—KidsHealth
http://www.kidshealth.org/kid/stay_healthy/fit/fat_thin.html

Glossary

calcium: a part of some foods that keeps teeth and bones healthy

energy: power within the body that lets it move and be active

healthy: being in good condition physically and mentally or something that helps you stay in good condition

minerals: something found in food that keeps us healthy. Calcium is a mineral.

oxygen: something people take in when they breathe. Living things need oxygen.

poultry: birds raised for their eggs and meat

protein: something in foods that helps keep muscles and other parts of your body healthy and strong

variety: a mix of different things

vitamins: a part of food that keeps us healthy and helps our body work

Index

eating the right amount, 16, 18–25

energy from food, 7, 26, 28

food groups, 4, 5, 17, 28

fruits group, 9, 21

grains group, 6, 7, 18, 19, 28

keeping active, 25–27

meat and beans group, 14, 23, 24

milk group, 12, 22

minerals, 10, 13, 28

MyPyramid, 4, 17, 29

oils group, 15, 25

variety, 5, 27

vegetables group, 8, 20, 28

vitamins, 10, 11, 28

Photo Acknowledgments

The photographs in this book appear courtesy of: © Ryan McVay/Getty Images, front cover; © Sam Lund/Independent Picture Service, p. 3; PhotoDisc Royalty Free by Getty Images, pp. 4, 8, 9, 11, 13, 26; © Royalty-Free/CORBIS, pp. 5, 7, 16; © Comstock/SuperStock, pp. 6, 12, 14; © Todd Strand/Independent Picture Service, pp. 10, 15, 17, 18, 19, 20, 23, 25; U.S. Department of Agriculture, pp. 21, 29; © Stock Image/SuperStock, p. 22; © age fotostock/SuperStock, p. 24; © Charles Gupton/CORBIS, p. 27.